STAY CURIOUS AND INSPIRED WITH WEEKLY LESSONS, STORIES, BOOKS, AND ACTIVITIES WITH TASHLULTUM THE AUTHOR EMAILS

JOIN OUR HUB TODAY AND UNLOCK A WORLD OF KNOWLEDGE AND POSSIBILITIES FOR YOUR STUDENTS.

THE JOURNEY TO QUALITY EDUCATION STARTS HERE!

- AMPLIFYING THE VOICES OF BLACK AMERICANS
- CONNECTING AND UNITING DIVERSE CULTURAL PERSPECTIVES

AF489297

A *Curious Question*

Meet Lily, a bright and curious young girl. She loves learning about history and the heroes who fought for justice. One day, she stumbles upon an old photo of a group of people wearing black berets and decides to ask her grandmother about it. Little does she know, this is the start of a remarkable journey through time.

The Beginning

Lily asks her grandma, "Who were the people in this picture wearing those cool black berets?" Grandma smiles and begins to tell Lily the story of the Black Panther Party. She paints a vivid picture of the 1960s, a time when things weren't fair for everyone. Lily learns that the Black Panther Party was started by young people who wanted to make the world a better place. They were like superheroes in their community.

Taking a
Stand

The Black Panthers believed
that everyone deserved
equal rights and that no
one should be treated
unfairly because of the
color of their skin. Lily feels
inspired by their bravery
and determination. She
learns about their courage
in the face of injustice and
discrimination.

Panther
Power

As Lily learns more, she
realizes that the Black
Panther Party used their
Panther Power to stand
against unfair treatment
and to protect their
community.

They taught people about their rights and made sure everyone had a voice. Lily starts to understand that speaking up for what's right is a powerful way to create positive change.

Challenges and Change

Lily discovers that the Panthers faced many challenges and even some misunderstandings. But they kept on fighting for justice and making their community a better place. She learns that making a difference isn't always easy, but it's worth the effort.

Leaving a Legacy

Lily's grandma tells her that although the Black Panther Party is no longer active, their legacy lives on. The ideas and values they fought for still inspire people today to stand up for what's right. She explains that it's important to remember and honor the people who came before us and made the world a better place.

Lily's Promise

Feeling inspired by the Black Panthers, Lily decides to make a promise. She'll use her own Panther Power to stand up for fairness, equality, and kindness in her community. She understands that even a young person like her can make a big difference by treating others with respect and standing up against injustice.

The Freedom Schools

As Lily continues her journey through the remarkable history of the Black Panther Party, her grandmother shares another incredible chapter: the story of the Freedom Schools.

Lily's eyes widen with curiosity as she listens to her grandmother's tale of these unique schools that were part of the Panther's commitment to education and empowerment. it.

The Panthers believed that knowledge was a powerful tool for change, and they wanted to ensure that everyone had access to it.

In the heart of the civil rights movement, the Panthers set up Freedom Schools to provide education to African American children and adults. These schools were open to all, but they aimed to empower black communities and equip them with the knowledge and skills to challenge the injustices they faced.

Lily learns that the curriculum in these schools wasn't just about reading, writing, and arithmetic. It also included lessons on black history, political awareness, and self-respect. The Panthers wanted everyone to understand their rights and to be proud of their heritage.

The impact of the Freedom Schools was immense. They inspired a thirst for knowledge and a hunger for change. Students, both young and old, came out of these schools not only with academic skills but also with a renewed sense of self-worth and a determination to fight for justice.

Lily's grandmother tells her and her friends that the legacy of the Freedom Schools is a testament to the Panthers' commitment to education and equality. They believed that education was the key to unlocking the chains of injustice, and the Freedom Schools were a powerful tool in that mission.

As Lily and her sister absorb this chapter of history, she realizes that education is indeed a potent weapon. She's grateful for the legacy of the Freedom Schools and the important role they played in the fight for justice and equality.

Inspired, Lily is eager to continue her
own journey of learning and to carry
the torch of knowledge forward in her
community.

Lily's journey through history has taught her that even young people can make a big difference. She's excited to share the story of the Black Panther Party with her friends and family and keep their legacy alive.

By learning about the values of community care, equality, and standing up for justice, she knows she can be a hero in her own way.

As Lily absorbs this chapter of history, she realizes that education is indeed a potent weapon. She's grateful for the legacy of the Freedom Schools and the important role they played in the fight for justice and equality. Inspired, Lily is eager to continue her own journey of learning and to carry the torch of knowledge forward in her community.

Lily's journey through history has taught her that even young people can make a big difference. She's excited to share the story of the Black Panther Party with her friends and family and keep their legacy alive. By learning about the values of community care, equality, and standing up for justice, she knows she can be a hero in her own way.

The Freedom Schools

In the heart of the civil rights movement, the Panthers set up Freedom Schools to provide education to African American children and adults. These schools were open to all, but they aimed to empower black communities and equip them with the knowledge and skills to challenge the injustices they faced.

Lily learns that the curriculum in these schools wasn't just about reading, writing, and arithmetic. It also included lessons on black history, political awareness, and self-respect. The Panthers wanted everyone to understand their rights and to be proud of their heritage.